If I'm Saved Why Is My Life Still a Mess?

How to Live Successfully as a Child of God

FOR NEW AND OLD DISCIPLES

MoriEl Randolph

ISBN: 978-0-9909090-5-7

CONTENTS

PREFACE

As the choir sings and the music plays, the pastor or priest invites you to come forward. The Spirit is strong, and the atmosphere is inviting as you listen to the words from the pulpit to come—come accept Jesus into your life and be saved. So you go, eyes flooded with tears and your heart full of hope.

The next day, it's back to work. You're hit with all the normal challenges of the day, but you've been told that you're born again and things should be different now. Days turn into weeks and weeks into months. Before you know it, years have passed, and your life is as big a mess as it was when you answered that call from the pulpit. Your belief in God hasn't changed, but neither has your life. You don't understand why or what you're supposed to do about it.

Well, first of all, know that you are among thousands who think and feel the same way. Many people are asking, "If I'm saved, why is my life still a mess?"

You will find the answer to that question within the pages of this book if what you read is received with a love for the truth.

WHAT A MESS!

As of this book's publishing date many statistics show that Christianity (consisting of those who profess to be followers of the Christ) is still the largest belief system in the world. Therefore, a vast number of individuals agree that there is only one Creator and Sovereign of the universe, and He has only one begotten Son. Such believers also know and believe that there is only one book sanctioned by our Creator, and it has been preserved to teach human beings about the Almighty and His Son. That book is called the Holy Bible. Everything else written regarding Christianity, or following the Christ, is supposed to be based on that one book.

Most with even the slightest interest in the truth are aware of the basic message and teachings of the Holy Bible. Yet there are more than forty denominations or divisions among those who claim to be followers of the Christ, and even more conflicting doctrines and teachings on the subject.

What we have is a mess!

This mess came about due to the fact that many people who believe in a Creator want what He has to offer, but they want it on their own terms. They may be willing to go along with portions of what He teaches, but when it comes to those things to which they're not willing to submit, they will find some way to falsely justify their disobedience.

People who believe in the Almighty and His Son generally believe in the authority of His Word as revealed in the Holy Bible. For this reason, they're not going to be comfortable with admitting to the Almighty that they're OK with only parts of His instructions. Nor are they willing to be honest with Him, or themselves, regarding the changes they wish to and do make when it comes to His Word (i.e., His thoughts, desires, commands, likes, dislikes, etc.). So they allow themselves to be deceived into seeing or hearing His instructions according to their own agendas. In fact, they sometimes manage to accept the complete opposite from what is preserved in the written Word of the Almighty.

This habit is nothing new. It's been going on from the beginning. The disciples wrote regularly about the problem and about the confusion and evil it causes. What really make this practice and the mess it's created so evil are the obstacles it creates for those who want to know the truth. It's also a hindrance to those who might get their acts together if their only choice for fellowship is with assemblies and teachers of the Word who stand by the truth, regardless of the cost.

The book you are now reading was written to lay out the unadulterated truth before you. It presents a step-by-step, clear, and simple guide detailing what it takes to live successfully as a child of the Most High through His Son, specifically in this day and age. If you find yourself objecting to its content, or looking for excuses to not accept what's written, then there is a great possibility that you are among those described above.

In spite of all the divisions or denominations, the Almighty is not confused. He has a system, a process, through which He takes all of His children in order to prepare them for their purpose in this age and for the age to come.

You would do well to read this book and simply be honest with yourself and with God if the truth is that you simply don't wish to adhere to the Almighty's process. What you are about to read is truly the way to live successfully in the Christ, whether you wish to accept it or not.

Denial does not negate the Truth; it never has, and it never will.

So before you begin to read, please examine yourself, count the cost, and make sure you want to know, because it is better to not know than to know and not do. The ultimate consequence is the same, but the eternal regret is far greater for those who knew but chose to reject or neglect the truth.

Now, before we get started, there are a few things you should take note of regarding the manner in which this book has been written:

This, and all portions of this publication, was written by an author who believes in the truth according to what the Almighty has preserved within the pages of what's known as the Holy Bible.

The titles used for the Almighty are many. We realize that the most popular of His titles is "God," but we have chosen to use other titles as well, such as Almighty and Creator.

INTRODUCTION

I was speaking to a woman about taking certain precautions should she end up needing long-term care. Her reply was that she trusted God would keep her healthy enough to avoid the need for long-term care. I replied, "If you expect Him to do that, He would appreciate it if you would stop smoking."

Too often, believers in the Almighty and His Son read His Word (i.e., the Bible) but somehow don't get the fact that we can actually hinder the Sovereign of the universe. A parent may have plans for his or her child, something the parent knows will bring the child great delight, only to be hindered by a choice the child makes or by the child's behavior.

How often did the Christ and His disciples use the relationship between earthly parents and their children to help us understand our position as children of the Most High?

Many times we chalk up what we're going through to trials, tribulations, or testing. Those who are suffering or enduring pain or torment for righteousness sake know who they are, and the Almighty's power, comfort, strengthening, or "grace" is sufficient for them. But in most cases, the suffering, problems, or troubles we endure result from our own choices and actions. The sooner we see and accept our responsibility or contribution to the condition of our lives, the sooner we can do something about it.

There is a process by which the Almighty rears His children. The problem is that most refuse (be it with or without awareness) to go through this process.

It's a lot like going to school or college. Though many are enrolled, many do not graduate, or in the words of our Teacher, "Many are called, but few chosen" (Matt. 20:16 NKJV).

However, in the Almighty's school, you don't get to pick and choose which classes you wish to take or the order in which you wish to take them—no more than an infant has a choice as to when he or she will become a toddler or a preschooler.

All of the courses are mandatory and must be taken according to His purpose. Those who wish to omit, pick, and choose what they will and will not do never complete the process. Thus they find themselves living spiritually weak and, many times, miserable lives. For many, this state leads to despair, a loss of hope, and, eventually, total defeat.

The following pages will walk you through the process. Use the content to examine your life thoroughly. As you read, ask yourself if you have neglected or run away from any aspect of His process. Have you thwarted your own growth?

If you wish to get on, or back on, track, then read this book carefully and accept and then apply the truth therein; not according to what you may be hearing from the pulpit or what you see other believers doing today but according to the life of the One who was given to us as our example to follow—the only begotten Son of the Almighty.

Caution: As you read the following chapters, you may find yourself thinking that I am a proponent of *Legalism*, or salvation by works instead of grace. I can assure you, I am not an advocate of either school of thought, and neither is this book. But if you find yourself having a hard time accepting that declaration, please make sure your doubt is not due to complacency, conviction, or a basic resistance to change.

1

THE COMMITMENT

PART I

Regardless of the degree or amount of knowledge one has, if one believes a superior being is responsible for the presence of humans on this earth, then one believes God exists. However, the person may not know who or what God is. The writer of Hebrews said, "And without faith it is impossible to please *God*, because anyone who comes to *him* must believe that *he* exists and that he rewards those who earnestly seek *him*" (Heb. 11:6, emphasis mine). The book of Romans also tells us, "since what may be known about *God* is plain to them, because *God* has made it plain to them. For since the creation of the world *God's* invisible qualities—*his* eternal power and divine nature—have been clearly seen, being understood from what has been made, so that people are without excuse (1:19–20, emphasis mine).

Every human being who lives long enough will come to a point in life when he or she will have to make a choice where the Almighty is concerned. We all will make this choice, whether we allow ourselves to be aware or not. Those who are aware of the choice to be made but choose to be what's called *agnostic*, while putting forth no effort to seek God, will fall under the same category as those who rejected Him if they continue to be "on the fence" throughout their lives.

In our culture today (at least in the United States) we have a "church" virtually on every corner, each one claiming to know God. In addition, for most, someone who had a part in our upbringing has shared with us his or her thoughts or beliefs regarding the Almighty and His Son.

Regrettably, having suppositions, preconceived ideas, or knowledge regarding God can actually make seeking Him harder than if one knew nothing.

The point is, if the knowledge shared was not accurate, then one must learn and discern what is and isn't true and then go through the process of dismissing what one has believed his or her entire life. That process is very uncomfortable but necessary if he or she truly wishes to know truth according to the Father of truth. This goal is challenging enough without a number of preconceived ideas getting in the way.

> For most, believing in the Supreme Being is not difficult.

Nevertheless, for most, believing in the Supreme Being is not difficult unless you are someone who would feel obligated to give allegiance to your Creator. But in your heart of hearts you simply do not want to. So what do you do? The answer is, you somehow allow yourself to be convinced that He does not exist. That way you can think you're not accountable and thus live your life as if you don't have to answer to Him.

Or you may be someone who is prideful or arrogant enough to think you can judge the Almighty based on what you see going on in the world, or because of some terrible, painful experience or loss in your own life. In this case, you choose to judge Him to be nonexistent because you don't approve of how the world is being run or things He "allows to happen."

The truth is, anyone who thinks like the above is unaware that God is not running this world. If He were, it would not be in the condition it's in. He's just preserving it for His ultimate purpose, and intervening where necessary, in order to make sure that His purpose is fulfilled (see Luke 4:4–8; 2 Corinthians 4:4; Ephesians 2:2).

The above types of thinking are what give birth to atheism.

Nevertheless, the vast majority believes in a Creator. So it just becomes a matter of getting to know who, what, and the way He is. However, one's belief has to be followed by a commitment to get to know Him, to develop a relationship with Him, and to live life as He (the Creator) intended. The problem is many do not know or understand how to commit to God. The truth be told, in this day and age many do not know how to commit to anything or anyone, nor are they willing to learn. A true commitment requires what most are not ready or willing to give. It requires *effort, determination,* and *perseverance*; and in most cases, it requires *discipline.*

Most people only give enough or do enough to get by. It is rare today to find truly committed individuals. The general mentality is "if the going gets tough, who needs it," hence the growing divorce rate in North America.

In our day, when individuals decide to commit to the Almighty, there's a very good possibility they have never had the experience of committing to anything or anyone their entire lives. So they must learn what it means and what it takes to make a commitment. More importantly, they must apply what they've learned.

Learning to commit will be just one of many things a believer will have to understand and apply in order to replace a multitude of old habits and ways *if* one truly wishes to live successfully as a child of God.

Ephesians 4:22–24 states, "You must put off old habits and former ways of thinking, which are corrupt because of former deceits and lusts. You must be renewed in your thinking and ways. You must put on new ways of thinking and form new habits which *the Sovereign* approves" (author's paraphrase). In order to accomplish that, it is absolutely necessary that we understand not only what a commitment is but also how to fulfill a commitment to the Almighty.

To commit to God, one must first believe that He exists and believe in the truth regarding His child He begot (i.e., Jesus, or Yehoshua). But in order to be successful, and to persevere in our commitment, we must also do the following:

- Believe and develop total trust in the writings the Almighty has preserved for those with a love for the Truth (i.e., the Bible) above all other resources.
- Accept and exercise the fact that He can do no wrong or make no mistakes.
- Accept and exercise the fact that no one knows better than the Almighty what is best for the life He's given you, in all things.
- Believe He will always do and permit that which is for your highest good.
- Accept and further develop your belief that He is trustworthy and, therefore, can be totally trusted to govern your life.
- Accept that you cannot govern your life correctly or righteously without Him, His Word, and His guidance.
- Believe that what occurs or does not occur in your life is good—if, and as long as, you are obedient and living life His way and according to His purpose.

In order to live in this world successfully as a child of God, you must be content and totally ready to submit to His way, accepting and believing that His way is the only way you should live.

You must long for nothing more than the freedom to obey Him and live life the way He intended. Once you have submitted to accepting and believing all of the above, through that very *belief* you will receive the power of the Holy Spirit from the Almighty and can put on and make use of the full armor of God:

> Finally, be strong in the Lord and in his mighty power. Put on the full armor of God, so that you can take your stand against the devil's schemes. For our struggle is not against flesh and blood, but against the rulers, against the authorities, against the powers of this dark world and against the spiritual forces of evil in the heavenly realms. Therefore put on the full armor of God, so that when the day of evil comes, you may be able to stand your ground, and after you have done everything, to stand. Stand firm then, with the belt of truth buckled around your waist, with the breastplate of righteousness in place, and with your feet fitted with the readiness that comes from the gospel of peace. In addition to all this, take up the shield of faith, with which you can extinguish all the flaming arrows of the evil one. Take the helmet of salvation and the sword of the Spirit, which is the word of God. (Eph. 6:10–17)

For the sake of clarity, I interchanged the words *accept* and *believe* in the above bullet points. However, to believe is to accept something or someone as true. The Almighty knows that when we first come to Him, other than what we've read about Him, He's somewhat of a stranger to us on a personal level. He knows it is a new relationship, and like all new relationships, trust must develop and grow, especially when that trust is in someone we cannot see with the physical eye.

Yet based on the evidence we have that He exists, we are expected to believe (i.e., accept) the truth He has preserved for us in His written Word. For those longing for the truth, the Bible speaks to the heart and cannot be denied. But our trust still grows over time, through the *personal* experiences we have with Him through His Son.

We will always continue to believe and hope for the life and age to come. But what we believe regarding our Father develops into more than just belief; it becomes what we know. It becomes a personal, intimate relationship built on a sound trust in Him. Eventually, it's based not just on what we've read or accepted in the beginning; eventually, it's based on the personal experiences we've had with our Father through His Son. These personal experiences are what give us the conviction and boldness to share our testimonies and His love with others.

The Spirit is willing, but the body is weak.

Within each individual who commits to the Almighty is a memory system filled with old memories, knowledge, habits, and programming to which the body is accustomed. The fact that old habits and behaviors are a part of you, and have been for a long time, means *you will feel discomfort in the beginning.* You will be faced with opportunities to choose between the new way of thinking or falling back into the old. When you choose the new, you will begin the process of forming new habits and new ways of thinking. But make no mistake—in the beginning, the old way will *feel* better. In Luke's gospel, Jesus said, "And no one after drinking old wine wants the new, for they say, 'The old is better'" (5:39).

The new knowledge and understanding we acquire will often cause conflicting thoughts or opposition within us. Nevertheless, in order to fulfill our commitment, we must strive daily to walk in obedience to God in spite of the conflicts. This is just one of the reasons why we must *long* to do things His way. If we have the longing, He has the power, and therefore it can be done. We can successfully live according to His purpose.

However, many choices we face will often cause the bodies we reside in to *feel* absolutely miserable. It's almost as if it throws a tantrum whenever we dare to even think about not giving it what it's accustomed to. In short, the Almighty can enable our thoughts to coincide with our longing to do what's right or good, but our bodies can *feel* the exact opposite. In other words, there will be conflict and resistance within you in the beginning. Let me stress those three words again—*in the beginning.* Putting off the old can be likened to going through drug withdrawal. However, addicts who are truly committed to freedom from drugs will commit to doing whatever it takes to get clean no matter how much pain or suffering they have to endure from their bodies. They will enlist whatever help is necessary to achieve their goal. They *persevere* because they are *determined*, a key requirement for any commitment. Those addicts who don't persevere go back to the very thing they said they wanted to be freed from, which is what many people do where the Almighty is concerned.

> Many choices we face will often cause the bodies we reside in to *feel* absolutely miserable.

The bottom line is this: in order to fulfill a commitment to God, you have to fight, resist, and disregard what you may *feel* in your body whenever it is opposed to what your God-enabled thoughts are saying. Depending on how great a hold the old habit has on you, you may need to practice this process over and over again until the old habit(s) is replaced by your God-inspired new habit(s). This process is made absolutely clear within the letter written by Paul to the disciples in Rome:

> Therefore, brothers and sisters, we have an obligation—but it is not to the flesh, to live according to it. For if you live according to the flesh, you will die; but if by the Spirit you put to death the misdeeds of the body, you will live.
>
> For those who are led by the Spirit of God are the children of God. (Rom. 8:12–14)

The Almighty Sovereign is trustworthy. If you long for righteousness, while asking and trusting Him to make you righteous, He will do it. He will convict you and bring to your attention the right thing to do or warn you not to do the wrong. He will provide you with one who is older than you "spiritually" to help you when you don't know what to do.

For example, a man wants to do what is good and right in order to please his Father in heaven, but he finds himself in a situation where he sees or meets someone who his body instantly responds to. When this happens old inclinations come forward, and his feet move to walk toward the woman or his mouth opens to engage in conversation. Immediately, by use of the Almighty's Enabling Power, or Holy Spirit, his Sovereign-enabled thoughts come forward telling him to remember Joseph and get away from the woman as quickly as possible. If he doesn't know, or has not read, the account of Joseph, his warning system, or conscience, warns him that he's headed for trouble.

In this scenario, one who is truly committed would be compelled to submit to his God-enabled thoughts or warnings. Even if he needed to pray or call someone for moral support, the committed individual would do whatever it takes to not give in, knowing that this particular weakness could cause him to transgress or sin against the Almighty. However, evil can be persistent, depending on one's longings, ambitions, flaws, or weaknesses:

> When tempted, no one should say, "God is tempting me."
> For God cannot be tempted by evil, nor does he tempt
> anyone; but each person is tempted when they are dragged
> away by their own evil desire and enticed. Then, after desire
> has conceived, it gives birth to sin; and sin,
> when it is full-grown, gives birth to death.
> (James 1:13–15)

An opposing force may suggest that he can't let this woman walk out of his life because the woman may be sent by God. It's for this reason that it's important to take time to learn from those who are further along the straight and narrow path. Someone who knows the ways and character of the Almighty can help you to discern God's leading until you are mature enough in Him to discern on your own.

In the above scenario, the man may need some-one who knows and trusts the Almighty well enough

It's important to take time to learn from those who are further along the straight and narrow path.

to discern that God would not have warned the man or enabled him to recall Joseph's temptation with Potiphar's wife if the woman were sent from God. If the man is willing to trust and wait on the Almighty (no matter how tempting it may be to take matters into his own hands), then God will make the temptation regarding the woman abundantly clear.

2

THE COMMITMENT
PART II

In chapter 4 of Mark's gospel, we find a parable (or story) that Jesus told about a farmer sowing seed:

> Listen! A farmer went out to sow his seed. As he was scatter-
> ing the seed, some fell along the path, and the birds came
> and ate it up. Some fell on rocky places, where it did not have
> much soil. It sprang up quickly, because the soil was shallow.
> But when the sun came up, the plants were scorched, and they
> withered because they had no root. Other seed fell among
> thorns, which grew up and choked the plants, so that they did
> not bear grain. Still other seed fell on good soil. It came up,
> grew and produced a crop, some multiplying thirty, some sixty,
> some a hundred times. (vv. 3–8)

Jesus told how the Word, as the seed, is unable to become rooted and grounded except in the prepared earth (i.e., those who readily hear the Word, believe it, walk by its counsel, and are set free from the force of evil). The words of our teacher tell us exactly why it is absolutely necessary for one to totally commit to the Almighty if he or she is to live successfully as His child. Jesus points out that those who successfully walk the path of true righteousness not only hear and believe the Word but also walk by its counsel. In other words, they are obedient to it. A person cannot be truly obedient to the Almighty without first making a commitment to Him. (Review what is required to make a commitment in part I.) The Word cannot take root unless one is truly obedient. It's a process, a cycle.

In order to be set free from the force or influence of evil, the Word must be readily heard and believed, and then one must walk by its counsel (i.e., obey what the Almighty has taught him or her to do through His spokespeople—the most important one being His begotten Son).

2 Corinthians 9:13

Because of the service by which you have proved yourselves, others will praise God for the *obedience* that accompanies your confession of the gospel of Christ, and for your generosity in sharing with them and with everyone else. (italics mine)

James 2:17–20

In the same way, faith by itself, if it is not accompanied by action, is dead.

But someone will say, "You have faith; I have deeds."

Show me your faith without deeds, and I will show you my faith by my deeds. You believe that there is one God. Good! Even the demons believe that—and shudder.

You foolish person, do you want evidence that faith without deeds is useless?

One should also understand that commitment is not obedience, but the commitment becomes null and void without obedience.

For example, a drug addict commits to a drug rehabilitation facility, but once in the program, he or she decides not to obey all the rules and regulations. Therefore, the addict will not be successful, and his or her commitment into the facility becomes worthless. Thus because of the addict's disobedience, he or she will not be freed from the drug addiction and will remain a *slave* to the addiction.

It is the same when one commits to the Almighty through His begotten Son. A commitment is the first step, but His Word will never take root (i.e., have a true governing and powerful effect in one's life) unless his or her commitment is followed by obedience.

A commitment is *determining to do* whatever it takes. Obedience is *doing* whatever it takes per the Almighty's instructions for His children. Therefore, obedience is the fulfillment of one's commitment. Commitment is the car you buy for the journey, but obedience is the driver. Here's how it works:

A. Make a commitment: "Yes, I am going to do whatever it takes to be an obedient child of God." This is the attitude you should maintain at all times.

B. Obey the Word, taking advantage of the growth, wisdom, and experiences of those you read about in the Bible who have successfully walked the path of the Almighty and present believers walking His path ahead of you—those whose fruit show that they truly belong to and live for Him. Always keep in mind that when His Word is absolutely clear about anything, to disobey would be transgression against Him. In case you did not notice, that was a "period" at the end of the foregoing sentence.

C. Focus on making the best of each day one day at a time. Understand that discerning what is the good or right thing to do in every area of your life is a learning and growing *process*. You also grow in obedience and in your ability to discern what the Almighty is telling you to do in any given situation:

> But solid food is for the mature, who by constant use have trained themselves to distinguish good from evil. (Heb. 5:14)

> Do not conform to the pattern of this world, but be transformed by the renewing of your mind. Then you will be able to test and approve what God's will is—his good, pleasing and perfect will. (Rom. 12:2)

D. Let your trust in Him grow. The only way to know and experience the true validity and power of the *thoughts* and *intentions* of the Almighty is to start and remain obedient to what He has preserved for you in His written Word.

The Almighty gives us clear choices. He has done so throughout time. Throughout His Word, He tells His people, "If you will obey, then I will . . . ." Therefore, it stands to reason that we can only experience what He says He will do if we obey Him.

Most people never experience the amazing, awesome power of the Almighty in their lives because they are not obedient; they will not give Him rule over their lives. They confess Him with their mouths, but their hearts are far from Him (Isa. 29:13; Matt. 15:8; Mark 7:6). Yet somehow, they convince themselves that they are in control.

When we are obedient to the Founder of Life, He can effectively move and work in our lives. We can actually see the results of this power in our lives, and our trust in Him grows:

> If you remain in me and my words remain in you, ask whatever you wish, and it will be done for you. (John 15:7)

But how can these words be fulfilled if we do not obey God? James describes what can take place when we (who are not obedient) pray to Him:

> You desire but do not have, so you kill. You covet but you cannot get what you want, so you quarrel and fight. You do not have because you do not ask God. When you ask, you do not receive, because you ask with wrong motives, that you may spend what you get on your pleasures. (James 4:2–3)

When we are obedient to the Word, we can see the power of that Word unfolding in our lives, thus our confidence grows along with our trust in the Almighty, and His Word can take root in us.

So many times people say, "I prayed and asked God to help me, and He didn't answer my prayer." To which I ask, "Are you doing the things that would permit Him to help you?"

Let's say I need a thousand dollars, and someone tells me, "Go up the street to the first house *on the left*, knock on the door, ask for Jim, he will give

When we are obedient to the Founder of Life, He can effectively move and work in our lives.

you the money." If I go up the street to the first house *on the right*, knock on the door, and ask for Jim, I am not going to get the money.

Let's say I doubt that what the person tells me to do will actually result in my getting a thousand dollars, but I follow the person's directions to the letter. Not only will I get the thousand dollars, but I am going to have a lot more confidence in what that person has to say should he or she give me instructions in the future.

The Christ went on to say, "These things I have spoken to you, that My joy may remain in you, and that your joy may be full" (John 15:11 NKJV).

The joy, peace, and hope that one experiences when he or she walks the Almighty's path according to His Word and His Way is the reason why those who live a life of obedience endure whatever the enemy throws their way. Paul said it best in his letter to the disciples in Rome:

> The Spirit you received does not make you slaves, so that you live in fear again; rather, the Spirit you received brought about your adoption to sonship. And by him we cry, "Abba, Father." The Spirit himself testifies with our spirit that we are God's children. Now if we are children, then we are heirs—heirs of God and co-heirs with Christ, if indeed we share in his sufferings in order that we may also share in his glory.
>
> I consider that our present sufferings are not worth comparing with the glory that will be revealed in us. (Rom. 8:15–18)

Yes, nothing in this world can be compared to the joy, hope, and peace we can receive from Him, but it is only truly experienced by those who are obedient to the Almighty (i.e., His obedient children) and those who put their trust in the Almighty. It all *must* begin with commitment.

You will be committing to God through His only begotten Son. It is a joyous cycle. The more you obey, the more you trust; the more you trust, the more you obey. As John H. Sammis wrote in his inspiring hymn we are to:

> Trust and obey, for there's no other way
> > to be happy in Jesus, but to trust and obey.

So by now you may be asking, "Then if I'm saved, why do I keep sinning? Why don't I obey Him when I know I should?"

Just keep reading; you may find the answer as you learn more about the day-to-day transition from sinner to saint, and the Almighty's process for all His children.

3

THE TRANSITION

PART I

With the exception of the Christ, everyone starts out in this world by default as a child of the opposer, due to the disobedience (i.e., submission to the ways and thinking of the opposer of God) by the first two humans and every accountable human born thereafter.

All humans are born with bodies that are tainted and vulnerable to the compelling force or influence of evil. From the first day of one's life, information is stored in the memory system and habits are formed. Thus one is literally programmed with the ways of the world. The degree or level of that programming has a lot to do with the type of parents, guardians, or other influences one may have throughout his or her upbringing. Each individual gains experiences and memories from the people he or she is exposed to, including teachers, acquaintances, TV characters, and members of one's kindred.

Then there's also the genetic programming our bodies acquire, such as blood type, nervous system, DNA, and so forth. We'll get more into the body and its habits later, but for now let's focus on mental programming—information, teachings, directions, habits, traditions, examples, and rituals—in short, information and practices we accept and make a part of our way of thinking, which determines the way we live our lives.

With each year that we live within these bodies, we are accumulating and storing this type of programming continually. Then the day comes when God, in His infinite mercy and compassion, through His Son, calls us to freedom:

> As for you, you were dead in your transgressions and sins, in which you used to live when you followed the ways of this world and of the ruler of the kingdom of the air, the spirit who is now at work in those who are disobedient . . . But because of his great love for us, God, who is rich in mercy, made us alive with Christ even when we were dead in transgressions—it is by grace you have been saved. (Eph. 2:1–2, 4–5)

To answer His call means to come to the Sovereign just as you are, but with one major change. That change is in the way you think and your attitude.

You no longer want to be the way you are. In other words, you no longer wish to remain a child of the opposer or in bondage to him; instead, you wish to belong to the Almighty who called you through His Son.

However, we must put the emphasis on the word *you*. *You* wish to belong to the Almighty, but that has nothing to do with your body or the programming that your memory system has been saturated with. In essence, when you answer His call, you are to come to Him ready and willing to do everything He says, but you come to Him with all the baggage of your former programming.

Imagine yourself standing before the Almighty in answer to His call with all your worldliness still clinging to you. What's the first thing you would do if a child, to whom you extended an invitation to live with you, came to your door ready, willing, and eager to live in your home and by your rules, but the child was dripping with filth? Of course you would escort him or her straight to the bathtub.

Paul writes about purifying ourselves to both the disciples in Corinth and Ephesus:

> Therefore, since we have these promises, dear friends, let us purify ourselves from everything that contaminates body and spirit, perfecting holiness out of reverence for God. (2 Cor. 7:1)

and,

> Husbands, love your wives, just as Christ loved the church and gave himself up for her to make her holy, cleansing her by the washing with water through the word, and to present her to himself as a radiant church, without stain or wrinkle or any other blemish, but holy and blameless. (Eph. 5:25–27)

By now you may be thinking, how does He cleanse us, and what am I supposed to do? Think of it this way: our Father gives us the soap and water we need, but we have to use it if we wish to be clean. The Almighty gives us everything we need through His Son, Jesus; that is, to live righteously— to put off the old programming, ways, and habits—and replace them with new ways and new habits that allow us to follow the example of the Christ. He enables us with power to resist our body's unwholesome yearnings. But if we've been given a lamp and the power needed for the lamp to light a room, what good will it do if we never turn the lamp on? The New Testament writers addressed this subject.

Romans 8:12–14

Therefore, brothers and sisters, we have an obligation—but it is not to the flesh, to live according to it. For if you live according to the flesh, you will die; but if by the Spirit you put to death the misdeeds of the body, you will live.

For those who are led by the Spirit of God are the children of God.

Ephesians 6:13–17

Therefore put on the full armor of God, so that when the day of evil comes, you may be able to stand your ground, and after you have done everything, to stand. Stand firm then, with the belt of truth buckled around your waist, with the breastplate of righteousness in place, and with your feet fitted with the readiness that comes from the gospel of peace. In addition to all this, take up the shield of faith, with which you can extinguish all the flaming arrows of the evil one. Take the helmet of salvation and the sword of the Spirit, which is the word of God.

Philippians 2:12–13

Therefore, my dear friends, as you have always obeyed—not only in my presence, but now much more in my absence—continue to work out your salvation with fear and trembling, for it is God who works in you to will and to act in order to fulfill his good purpose.

Hebrews 13:20–21

Now may the God of peace, who through the blood of the eternal covenant brought back from the dead our Lord Jesus, that great Shepherd of the sheep, equip you with everything good for doing his will, and may he work in us what is pleasing to him, through Jesus Christ, to whom be glory for ever and ever. Amen.

His Word makes it clear that He gives us what we need, but if we really want to be free and live according to His purpose, then we have to make use of what He gives us.

Our Father permits us to experience certain situations so we can see the good, bad, and the ugly within ourselves. With that insight and understanding, we know why we need the "soap and water." He will also permit certain events in our lives so we may see if particular areas have been successfully cleansed. Because it is God "who works in you to will and to act in order to fulfill his good purpose," we don't have to worry about what we need to experience or encounter in order to grow in Him. As usual, He's got that all under control.

I cannot stress enough that the blood of Jesus cleanses us from the sin that alienated us from the Almighty. But, regarding our growth, the Bible uses words such as "purge," "prune," "put off," and "replace." That's because, once He makes us His own, He puts us through training to prepare us for His work and purpose and also for the kingdom and age to come. To complete His training, we must be active, willing participants. This is one of the reasons why the Bible is full of things we are told to do.

James 1:2–4

Consider it pure joy, my brothers and sisters, whenever you face trials of many kinds, because you know that the testing of your faith produces perseverance. Let perseverance finish its work so that you may be mature and complete, not lacking anything.

1 Peter 1:6

In all this you greatly rejoice, though now for a little while you may have had to suffer grief in all kinds of trials.

1 Peter 5:10–11

And the God of all grace, who called you to his eternal glory in Christ, after you have suffered a little while, will himself restore you and make you strong, firm and steadfast. To him be the power for ever and ever. Amen.

It is extremely important to understand that God's Word, His Enabling Power or Holy Spirit, His wisdom, favor, the life of His Son, and anything else He has to offer cannot help or enable us to become clean if we are not ready or willing to put forth the effort to wash (i.e., use what He gives us in obedience). We wash or clean up by:

- putting forth the consistent effort to replace old habits with new ones as the Almighty shows us the difference between the two;

- declaring war against anything *within us* that opposes what the Almighty teaches us through His Word;
- not only reading but also studying His Word in order to make it the guide for our lives on this earth;
- imagining Jesus with us at all times, and thereby developing the habit of thinking as He would think, acknowledging our heavenly Father in everything.

The cleansing process is just that, a process. No one is zapped clean. Jesus told His disciples that they were clean by way of the Word they were exposed to as they spent each day with Him. But this was told to them at the end of His ministry after they had spent at least three years with Him. It was not just the hearing of the Word that purged them; it was obedience to the Word. The point is, they walked with the Christ Himself. And still it took time—it was a process. The more worldly the programming and the deeper its influence, the longer the process may take.

We know and understand how long it takes for a human being to grow and mature physically. Yet when it comes to going from being totally worldly to a righteous and holy child of the Almighty, which means literally changing one's way of thinking and way of life or lifestyle, one rarely appreciates the process and the time it takes. The adoption into His kindred can take place in an instant, but prepping and training us to think and act like holy royalty takes a lifetime. It not only takes time, it takes perseverance. It takes effort and determination. This is why the Christ taught,

> The adoption into His kindred can take place in an instant.

"The one who stands firm to the end will be saved." (Matt. 10:22), and "To the one who conquers I will grant to eat of the tree of life, which is in the paradise of God" (Rev. 2:7 ESV).

Also see: Revelation 2:26; 3:5.

4

THE TRANSITION
PART II

You vs. Your Body

As was mentioned in chapter 1, when one answers the Almighty's call and then determines to do things His way, the decision has nothing to do with the mortal body he or she resides in while on this earth. Romans 8:6–7 tells us, "The mind governed by the flesh is death, but the mind governed by the Spirit is life and peace. The mind governed by the flesh is hostile to God; it does not submit to God's law, nor can it do so."

The body is not and cannot be subject to God. However, it is subject to the person who lives in it if he or she brings it into subjection. In order to do that, one must change the way one thinks about his or her body.

An effective way to accomplish this is to think of your body as a child: a child who has more than likely been spoiled (i.e., given into—a lot), a child who lacks discipline, a child who has gotten accustomed to having his or her own way and doing many things that are detrimental and against the Almighty.

However, the big difference between your body and an actual child is that when this child (i.e., your body) throws a tantrum, you can't send it to its room. You can't even go to another room in order to get away from it. You have to feel and experience whatever discomfort, turmoil, or pain the child (your body) may put you through. Like a child, your body will not submit to what you say or how you would have it behave until it knows you mean what you say and say what you mean.

Once you submit totally to the Almighty, you have to let your body know who is in charge. You have to make it absolutely clear that there is no use in throwing a tantrum or a fit because with the Enabling Power of God, through His Son, Jesus, you will not give into it.

The great news is, once your body knows that you are 100 percent determined, it will submit to you, whether it is gluttony, fornication, slothfulness, or any other unwholesome yearning.

Romans 13:13–14

Let us behave decently, as in the daytime, not in carousing and drunkenness, not in sexual immorality and debauchery, not in dissension and jealousy. Rather, clothe yourselves with the Lord Jesus Christ, and do not think about how to gratify the desires of the flesh.

Galatians 5:16–17

So I say, walk by the Spirit, and you will not gratify the desires of the flesh. For the flesh desires what is contrary to the Spirit, and the Spirit what is contrary to the flesh. They are in conflict with each other, so that you are not to do whatever you want.

However, most people either give in to the discomfort and eventually give up altogether, or find ways to falsely justify their choice. This is due to either spiritual laziness or cowardice or is because they were not truly determined in the first place, so it's not really worth it to them to endure. But in most cases it's because they are in empathy with their bodies. Here's an example of the latter.

Let's say a mother and her son are in a store that sells ice cream. Both the mother and the child are on a much-needed, low-fat diet. When the child sees the ice cream, he goes through several changes in order to get the mother to buy some.

The mother is endeavoring to hold her ground by saying no to the child, but the fact is she would like to have the ice cream as badly as the child. Who do you suppose will ultimately give in, the mother or the child?

Children instinctively know when a parent is susceptible. They also know by those same instincts when there is no use. Once a child knows that his or her parent is determined, the child gives in or gives up on whatever it is and submits.

> Most people either give in to the discomfort and eventually give up altogether, or find ways to falsely justify their choice.

The same applies to the body. One of the greatest challenges a child of the Almighty will face will be bringing his or her body into submission and dealing with its unwholesome yearnings. This is true especially in the beginning because the body is earthly; it doesn't have a lot to lose, and it is not subject to the Almighty's commands.

Like a child, or even a pet, it just wants to take its ease, have fun, and feel good. This is why it is so important to teach our children how to use their mind systems and develop discipline at a young age—because it's our intellect, our ability to think and reason, that separates us from the animals.

The vast majority of people when faced with the challenge of subduing their bodies will simply give in to whatever feels good or what is comfortable, and, therefore, they never succeed at becoming truly free from the force or influence of evil that compels the body.

Paul speaks of the power of the body, before conversion, in his letter to the disciples in Rome:

> For I do not do the good I want to do, but the evil I do not
> want to do—this I keep on doing. (Rom. 7:19)

It's obvious that Paul was not in empathy with his body.

This portion of the Scriptures describes perfectly the struggle we encounter when what we wish to do opposes what our bodies want to do or are in the habit of doing. It demonstrates the condition we are in and the struggle we encounter when we are still enslaved to the force or influence of evil in our lives.

Most people are not aware of where the conflict lies because they do not consider the fact that they are separate from their bodies, thus they believe that they are the cause for the entire problem.

However, anyone who wishes to live successfully as a child of God must understand that wishing or wanting to do the right thing is not enough. No matter how good a person's intentions may be, she must first determine that no matter how uncomfortable or miserable she may *feel*, she has to persevere until her body submits to what she wants, not the other way around. When that determination is coupled with the same power the Almighty used to raise His Son from the dead, you have amazing success! Deuteronomy 5:29 says, "Oh, that their hearts would be inclined to fear me and keep all my commands always, so that it might go well with them and their children forever!" The fact is, whether converted or unconverted, there are great benefits for anyone who succeeds at subduing his or her body, even if it's only in specific areas.

Let me stress again why this is: the body, by nature, is only interested in what feels good, tastes good, and is easy and comfortable. In fact, the body without the mind systems or spirit is just like an animal.

Animals have a brain—some even have the ability to feel—but as far as we know, they don't have a mind system or spirit (i.e., the part of an individual that remains after the body dies). Also, their intellectual capacity is little to nothing compared to that of humans.

One look at society reveals that only those who subdue their bodies (although only in specific areas) rise above the majority. These individuals are a small minority because the majority of society throughout the entire world is made of people who are slaves to their bodies and its yearnings, and what's worse, they're not even aware of it.

> The body, by nature, is only interested in what feels good, tastes good, and is easy and comfortable.

As for the minority of worldly-thinking people, who endure the pain or discomfort their bodies put them through in order to realize their goals, they are only victorious in the area(s) in which they subdue their bodies. In other areas, they permit their bodies to reign.

Just think of certain athletes who are controlled, efficient machines when it comes to their sport, but their personal lives are an absolute mess because of a bad temper or lack of control over their sexual urges.

There is a distinct difference between the unconverted that subdue their bodies in just some areas and the Almighty's children.

A child of God should know and understand that he or she must withstand and fight against the unwholesome desires of his or her body and unseen forces that can affect the body. His children should know that they have at their disposal whatever they need to achieve dominance over the body. They also should know that though the fight is hard, it prepares them for the eternal age to come, when they will inherit with Jesus everything the Creator has made. A child of God also should understand that the body is susceptible to many earthly things and, therefore, like a child, must be guarded.

> As children of the Most High, we must understand that the body's time is short.

As you think of your body as a child, also think about the fact that a good parent is always one step ahead of his or her child—knowing or discerning what would and would not be good to expose the child to depending on the child's age. A good parent knows not to permit his or her child to do or have anything that the child is not mature enough to handle, or that may lead the child to develop a bad or unhealthy habit.

A child of God must take the same care regarding his or her body. His children must remember that bad habits are easy to develop, and many good habits are easy to break. The body is a habitual vessel. It will develop habits, whether good or bad.

As children of the Most High, we must also understand that the body's time is short. The physical body has no eternal benefit. Therefore, if one's body is successful in getting its owner to submit to its yearnings, only the owner of that body will reap the eternal consequences. The body has very little to lose; it will simply return to the earth once it inevitably dies.

> ### Deuteronomy. 4:7–9 NKJV
> For what great nation is there that has God so near to it, as the Lord our God is to us, for whatever reason we may call upon Him? And what great nation is there that has such statutes and righteous judgments as are in all this law which I set before you this day? Only take heed to yourself, and diligently keep yourself, lest you forget the things your eyes have seen, and lest they depart from your heart all the days of your life. And teach them to your children and your grandchildren.

Children of God must accept and understand that they are not their bodies. They cannot permit their bodies to have rule over who and what they are and how they live their lives, especially since the opposer works through the body's weakness.

In essence, one cannot successfully live as a child of God without successfully ruling or bringing his or her body into total submission to the way God has determined His children should live.

If the Almighty rules over us, we must rule over our bodies using the knowledge provided for us within His Word and the enabling power He gives us with the receiving of His Holy Spirit, through our belief in His only begotten Son: Jesus.

It can be quite a struggle in the beginning, but for those who persevere, there is nothing on earth that can reap as great a benefit or reward. For in doing so, you gain your freedom to live the way God intended humans to live now and throughout eternity.

This is just one of the reasons for Paul's words to Timothy:

> If we endure,
>> We shall also reign with Him.
> If we deny Him,
>> He also will deny us. (2 Tim. 2:12 NKJV)

5

THE PROCESS
STEP I: SEPARATION

When one accepts the truth regarding life and its Founder, based on what's preserved within versions of the Holy Bible, and determines to make the Almighty the Ruler (i.e., the authority in his or her life), there is a process one must undergo. There are no exceptions; and most importantly, to omit any aspect of or to usurp the process would make success as a child of God impossible.

This chapter provides its readers with an in-depth understanding of what that process is. By understanding each step or aspect of the process, one can examine and follow his or her progress.

Though we may each progress at a different pace, there are basically five aspects, or steps, in the process. Each step eventually merges with the other. Some steps are single experiences taken over an extended period of time, while others are taken simultaneously. This is especially true of steps one and two. Though they should take place one after the other, these two steps may be taken in reverse.

One might say that the process is God's way of raising His children. As descendants of His creation, made in His likeness and image, we, too, use a process to raise our children—that is if we intend to be good and effective parents.

Likewise, any good educator or institution has a process for developing and teaching its students. So, of course, the same would be true of the Almighty when it comes to His children or disciples (i.e., students). He has a process for bringing His children to maturity and His students to completion.

We refer to these five steps as follows:

1. Separation
2. Immersion
3. Learning and Purging
4. Testing
5. Possession

This chapter is dedicated to step 1 of the process.

Separation

From the examples we find in God's Word, we see that separation is a definite requirement in order to successfully follow His ways and instructions and fulfill His purpose for our lives. However, one may ask, what type of separation, or separation from what? Let's look to the Word for those answers:

> Then the Lord said to Noah, "Come into the ark, you and all your household, because I have seen that you are righteous before Me in this generation. (Gen. 7:1 NKJV)

Most people know the account regarding Noah and the ark. But many may not recognize that when the Almighty enclosed Noah and his kindred in the ark, He separated Noah from all the other people in the world. This is a literal example of separation to the fullest degree. There are other examples of the Almighty separating His people.

> When Pharaoh heard of this, he tried to kill Moses, but Moses fled from Pharaoh and went to live in Midian, where he sat down by a well. (Ex. 2:15)

We know from the total account regarding Moses that his fleeing led him to Midian. This was God's way of separating Moses from the life and environment he knew in order to prepare him for the purpose God had for him.

Here is another example, this time involving Israel:

> The LORD said to Moses, "Consecrate to me every firstborn male. The first offspring of every womb among the Israelites belongs to me, whether human or animal."
>
> Then Moses said to the people, "Commemorate this day, the day you came out of Egypt, out of the land of slavery, because the LORD brought you out of it with a mighty hand." (Ex. 13:1–4)

In this passage, as with many aspects of the Word of the Almighty, He uses Israel as a physical example of the process and working of His plan of freedom.

The total account given in Exodus shows us that when the Israelites cried out, the Almighty sent His representative and set them free from their bondage. After taking them out of Egypt, He also gave them laws to keep them separate from the other worldly cultures of that day. The last example we shall use from the Old Testament is with Abraham:

> The LORD had said to Abram, "Go from your country, your people and your father's household to the land I will show you." (Gen. 12:1)

In this example, we see that God gave Abram (who He later renamed Abraham) a command. This command or requirement is what the Christ spoke of in the New Testament.

Matthew 10:37–39

He who loves father or mother more than Me is not worthy of Me. And he who loves son or daughter more than Me is not worthy of Me. And he who does not take his cross and follow after Me is not worthy of Me. He who finds his life will lose it, and he who loses his life for My sake will find it. (NKJV)

Mark 10:28–30

Then Peter spoke up, "We have left everything to follow you!" "Truly I tell you," Jesus replied, "no one who has left home or brothers or sisters or mother or father or children or fields for me and the gospel will fail to receive a hundred times as much in this present age: homes, brothers, sisters, mothers, children and fields—along with persecutions—and in the age to come eternal life."

Other examples from the New Testament are:

Luke 4:1 (regarding the Christ)

Jesus, full of the Holy Spirit, left the Jordan and was led by the Spirit into the wilderness.

Mark 1:20 (regarding the disciples)

Without delay he called them, and they left their father Zebedee in the boat with the hired men and followed him.

Galatians 1:15–19 (regarding Paul)

But when God, who set me apart from my mother's womb and called me by his grace, was pleased to reveal his Son in me so that I might preach him among the Gentiles, my immediate response was not to consult any human being. I did not go up to Jerusalem to see those who were apostles before I was, but I went into Arabia. Later I returned to Damascus.

Then after three years, I went up to Jerusalem to get acquainted with Cephas and stayed with him fifteen days. I saw none of the other apostles—only James, the Lord's brother.

2 Corinthians 6:17 (regarding all believers)

Therefore,
    "Come out from them
        and be separate,
            says the Lord.
    Touch no unclean thing,
        and I will receive you."

At this point, it is important to also explore the word *holy*, which according to the *New World Dictionary* means belonging to or coming from God. Also, in *Strong's Concordance* the word *consecrated* is included in the definition of holy, and it means to set apart for God.

The Almighty calls us to be holy: "But just as he who called you is holy, so be holy in all you do" (1 Pet. 1:15).

This explains why the first step we must take for freedom from the deceiver, his forces, and the ways of the world is separation. Just as the Almighty required that Israel leave Egypt after setting them free from the pharaoh's bondage, He also requires each and every person who claims to have a longing to know and belong to Him to be set aside (i.e., separated for His use and purpose). The separation is to place us in a position for transformation: a position that's necessary for anyone who truly wants to be a part of Him, under His rulership—a true child of God and follower of His Son, the Christ.

Think about it: if one lives in China and wishes to be governed by the United States and its laws, can he do so without leaving China and placing himself in a position to become a citizen of the United States?

But what about our family members?

Abraham was expected to leave his whole family with the exception of his wife for she would play a big role in God's plan. However, he dragged his nephew along, which appears to have been a mistake; thus, inevitably, he had to separate from him also.

In order to appreciate why the Almighty requires this step, you have only to ask yourself: Can I take my family members into training with me when joining the military? How often does one even see family members during basic training or wartime?

The Almighty requires that anyone who wishes to belong to Him and be under His rulership must separate himself or herself from anyone or anything that would get in the way of God's process for His children.

In the military, young men and women go to train for a responsibility that involves the saving and protecting of lives. So it is for God's soldiers. It is absolutely imperative that we free ourselves from old ties, old ways of thinking, and old influences. Paul told Timothy:

No one serving as a soldier gets entangled in civilian affairs,
but rather tries to please his commanding office. (2 Tim.2:4)

Therefore, if there is anyone or anything that would get in the way of our following the Christ (without distraction), especially while in basic training, then we must take heed to what He taught:

What I tell you in the dark, speak in the daylight; what is whispered in your ear, proclaim from the roofs. (Matt. 10:27)

Now you may think, I'm still in school and live with my parents. How could I go anywhere or separate from anyone? Physical separation, depending on circumstances, may not be required or may not be wise for some. This is something that one must petition the Almighty fervently about because the wrong choice could be a great stumbling block.

Furthermore, the Christ and his earlier disciples taught us that our heavenly Father and Ruler rules

> The Christ and his earlier disciples taught us that our heavenly Father and Ruler rules from within.

from within. Hence, for many, the physical separation from certain family members, or other influences, in our lives is not necessary. This may be due to the fact that the physical separation has already taken place, either due to adulthood or perhaps even the passing of a close family member.

Nevertheless, though not physical, separation is still necessary. The old programming of our parents, siblings, or even teachers is still within us, and, therefore, as the Word instructs us, we must put off the old and put on the new. We must replace what our parents, or others of the world, have taught us with what God has taught us through His Son, His spokespeople, or whomever else He may use. We should hold up everything we think we already know to the light of His Word in order to see if it coincides with His knowledge and understanding. It does not mean that everything we've been taught is wrong or bad. That's why we have to hold it up to His light. Jesus told His disciples, "Therefore every teacher of the law who has become a disciple in the kingdom of heaven is like the owner of a house who brings out of his storeroom new treasures as well as old" (Matt. 13:52).

In closing this chapter, the Word makes clear that the first step in the process designed to bring His children to maturity, and focused on the path that leads to eternal unity with God, is separation within; and many times, physical separation from whomever and whatever would hinder our progress. To forgo this step is to demonstrate from the start that one is not worthy to follow the Christ.

The reason Jesus could go so far as to make the very strong statement "is not worthy of Me" was because of what the Almighty offers. In Romans 8:18, Paul said, "I consider that our present sufferings are not worth comparing with the glory that will be revealed in us." He went on to say in Ephesians 3:20, "Now to him who is able to do immeasurably more than all we ask or imagine, according to his power that is at work within us."

The fact is, with all that God offers us and has done for us, and the fact that by Him we live and breathe and have being, there should be no one and nothing more important to us than our commitment and obedience to the Almighty; nor should there be anything more important than following every step He requires in His process designed to make and keep us holy and fit for His purpose, now and for the new age to come.

6

THE PROCESS
STEP II: IMMERSION (BAPTISM)

You've been set free by the Almighty (through His Son) from the pharaoh (who represents the deceiver, the chief opposer of God). The Almighty brought you out of Egypt (i.e., the world) by setting you apart. He did so because you were in bondage, a slave to the opposer. But just as the Israelites did when they were slaves in Egypt, you cried out to Him, believing that He, through His Son, could set you free.

Or did you?

The Almighty offers a new life, a new beginning for those who long to be free from who or what they are and what they've done. Though they may come to Him out of the fear of going to hell, fear alone will not keep them.

This is one reason why so many fail at walking the path that allows them to follow the Christ. "Many are called but few are chosen," (Matt. 22:14 NKJV), because most want what the Almighty has to offer, but they don't want the responsibility that comes with it.

You can find more detailed information regarding this hindrance on my blog at www.what-is-the-truth-today.com. The post is titled "About Salvation." I strongly recommend you take the time to read it.

The point is, if you initially come to God just out of reverence and fear, He can use that as an opportunity to show you your need for freedom, for a new life. Without an appreciation for what you've been saved from, you simply won't be able to stay the course (i.e., walk the straight and narrow); and, like most, you won't be able to endure to the end.

In order for this step to be effective, one must appreciate his or her need for a new life, the need to begin again, because the next step is just that—a new life. Starting one's life over as a new creation is a crucial and required part of His adoption process.

> We will have to drag our bodies (screaming and kicking) into submission as we strive each day to live in obedience to our Father in heaven.

For this step, God has actually established an outward and physical ritual. Just as the physical body comes through a mother's womb, God requires that those born of Him go through a formal procedure that symbolizes a new womb. This new womb gives birth to the new person we become.

This new birth has absolutely nothing to do with our physical bodies. In fact, in the beginning, we will have to drag our bodies (screaming and kicking) into submission as we strive each day to live in obedience to our Father in heaven. Review chapter four *The Transition, Part II*.

Step II of the process serves a threefold purpose. In addition to a symbolic womb, it also represents the death of the person you were, and it represents the victory brought about by His Son when He rose from the dead.

Romans 6:3–4

Or don't you know that all of us who were baptized into Christ Jesus were baptized into his death? We were therefore buried with him through baptism into death in order that, just as Christ was raised from the dead through the glory of the Father, we too may live a new life.

John 3:5–8

Jesus answered, "Very truly I tell you, no one can enter the kingdom of God unless they are born of water and the Spirit. Flesh gives birth to flesh, but the Spirit gives birth to spirit. You should not be surprised at my saying, 'You must be born again.' The wind blows wherever it pleases. You hear its sound, but you cannot tell where it comes from or where it is going. So it is with everyone born of the Spirit."

John 1:11–13

He came to that which was his own, but his own did not receive him. Yet to all who did receive him, to those who believed in his name, he gave the right to become children of God—children born not of natural descent, nor of human decision or a husband's will, but born of God.

The Almighty, as in most cases, used the Israelites first to demonstrate this step of the process:

For I do not want you to be ignorant of the fact, brothers and sisters, that our ancestors were all under the cloud and that they all passed through the sea. They were all baptized into Moses in the cloud and in the sea. (1 Cor. 10:1–2)

Above, we see where God, using Israel as an example, had them immersed all together shortly after He had delivered them from Egypt. However, the most important example of this step of the process is Jesus: "Jesus came from Galilee to the Jordan to be baptized" (Matt. 3:13). Before officially beginning His ministry, Jesus was immersed. He was sent to be our example.

It's important to interject here that the results of the outward act of immersion are supposed to have already taken place within the thoughts and minds of those who go through the ritual. As Paul stated in Romans 6 in his letter to the disciples in Rome, "knowing this, that our old man was crucified with Him, that the body of sin might be done away with, that we should no longer be slaves of sin" (v. 6 NKJV). The ritual is an outward manifestation of what should have already taken place within us.

Each person, *before* going through this ritual, should be able to appreciate, believe, understand, and agree with conviction the following:

- I want a new life.
- I want God to rule over my life.
- I want to live His way.
- I want to be as close to Him as possible.
- I realize that it should have been me *crucified*, or in our modern-day terminology *executed*, but the Christ died in my stead.
- I understand that I and all humans brought into this world have no right to live our lives with blatant disregard for the very Entity that gives us breath, by whom we move and live and have our being.

- I know that I have no right to do those things that God hates because of the pain and evil those things can cause myself and others.
- I accept that He cared enough to make it possible for me to have a relationship with Him by permitting His only born child that He brought into this world to suffer the shame, pain, and death that I and every human being deserved.
- I understand and appreciate that the Almighty watched His Son suffer execution because of the good it would do and the opportunity it would give humanity. I understand and appreciate that God was willing to do this in spite of the disregard humans have shown Him and His only begotten Son.
- I understand that because of Jesus's willingness to have His body die for me, and because of His victory over transgression and evil forces, I have been set free to come out of the water of my immersion with the authority and power to live a new life according to the purpose of the Almighty.
- I understand that my freedom was bought for a price that I could never repay.
- I understand that the freedom and abilities that have been given to me from God are gifts. However, I should live each day of my new life with a longing to live with and for God according to His purpose, and I would have it no other way.

Getting to know God and His way of doing things or how He wants things done is a long process, one that is not totally fulfilled until we're given immortality. Step two of the process is just the beginning.

Nevertheless, anyone who chooses to be immersed should not do so without embracing all of the above, for it contains the very foundation of His plan of freedom and the collective purpose for His adopted children.

Without accepting all of the above bullet points and our need for a new life, we cannot successfully follow the Christ. We have to see and accept not only that we need freedom but also what we need to be set free from. We need to see our need for salvation, but it is even more important that we understand why we have that need. It should not be just a verse that we quote from the Bible but a deep conviction and appreciation of who we were, what we've done, and the need to put our prior lives to death to be born anew.

7

THE PROCESS
STEP III: LEARNING AND PURGING

Steps three and four go hand in hand. But because one comes before the other, they are listed as two separate steps. Regrettably, these are the steps in the process that cause individuals the most difficulty. They're also the steps that most people fail to complete; and in doing so, many disrupt their unity with God.

> **2 Peter 3:17**
> Therefore, dear friends, since you have been forewarned, be on your guard so that you may not be carried away by the error of the lawless and fall from your secure position.

> **Hebrews 12:15**
> See to it that no one falls short of the grace of God and that no bitter root grows up to cause trouble and defile many.

Take heed, for too often we're not aware of our state because of deception or blindness due to who, or what, we've put before Him.

To teach regarding these steps in the process we will once again use the examples given to us through the Almighty's history with the Israelites (i.e., the descendants of Israel). The Israelites cried out to the Almighty while in bondage to Egypt. God set them free; He set them apart; He baptized them via the Red Sea; and He placed them in a position to live a new life with Him as their Ruler.

However, in His wisdom, He knew that after spending all those years in Egypt, they had to be purged. He knew they needed to get to know Him, His ways, and His laws. In other words, they had to be taught *how* to think and how to live the new life He had given them.

For the purging and learning process, He took them through the wilderness as He led them toward the promised land.

Their first destination: Mount Sinai. What was the purpose of going to the mount? To receive His laws.

There were people whose journey ended at the mount due to their rebellion and disobedience (see Exodus chapters 19–34). But those who moved on received His laws and were to complete their journey under God's guidance.

Everyone was supposed to apply His laws, obey His instructions, and reach the final destination according to His plan. But that's not what happened. Paul sums it up nicely:

> They all ate the same spiritual food . . . Nevertheless, God was
> not pleased with most of them; their bodies were scattered in
> the wilderness. (1 Cor. 10:3, 5)

Why was the Almighty not pleased? Why did many Israelites die in the wilderness instead of going on to the land God designated for them? Well, we could get into particulars and pick out all the things they did, or we could get right down to the root of their problem, the same problem many face today.

First, let's look at the fact that all who are set free and adopted by the Almighty through His Son go through their own personal wilderness, be it physical, spiritual, or both. Every single person who chooses the path of the Almighty takes this step in His process, including Jesus:

> Then Jesus was led by the Spirit into the wilderness to be tempted by the devil. (Matt. 4:1)

> All who are set free and adopted by the Almighty through His Son go through their own personal wilderness.

Paul also gives us an example of going through his wilderness:

> But when God, who set me apart from my mother's womb and called me by his grace, was pleased to reveal his Son in me so that I might preach him among the Gentiles, my immediate response was not to consult any human being. I did not go up to Jerusalem to see those who were apostles before I was, but I went into Arabia. Later I returned to Damascus. (Gal. 1:15–17)

The Israelites, Jesus, and Paul all experienced a physical wilderness; but for most people today, their wilderness march takes place within.

Those within God's household who have a discerning eye know when one of their spiritual siblings is going through this step in the process. They may not refer to it as the wilderness march, but they recognize the process of learning, testing, and purging within the life of a child of God.

For example, I know of someone who, during her wilderness march, literally went from one residence to another. In fact, during this period of her life, she moved eleven times in one year. However, it was not what took place around her that brought about these events; it was the conditions within her that influenced the decisions she made and the lessons she had to learn.

The point is, we all go through a growing and purging stage in the process that serves as our wilderness march. If we receive His ways and laws in obedience and simply follow His instructions, we will get through the wilderness and move on to the final step in the process.

Much like the Israelites, most of us today either spend far too much time in our wilderness or we die there.

So, getting back to the root of the problem, there are three basic reasons why this occurs. The Word does a great job of pointing them out for us. The writer of Hebrews tells us that God said,

> That is why I was angry with that generation;
>> I said, "Their hearts are always going astray,
>> and they have not known my ways." (3:10)

The key words are "they have not known my ways."

Hopefully, it is becoming clear that the Almighty indeed has a process, a certain way of doing things. The descendants of Israel had received His laws, precepts, decrees, and so forth. He gave them instructions on how to do everything. He practically took them by the hand to guide them through the wilderness towards their destination. All He asked of them was that they be obedient to do things His way.

But those who displeased God not only failed at doing things His way; they also weren't willing to put forth the effort to learn His ways. They held on to the old and rejected the new. Why? Because it was easier. And though they professed out of their mouths that they would have Him rule over them, in their stubbornness they refused to submit to His rulership:

> Therefore since it still remains for some to enter that rest,
> and since those who formerly had the good news proclaimed
> to them did not go in because of their disobedience, God
> again set a certain day, calling it "Today." This he did when
> a long time later he spoke through David, as in the passage
> already quoted:

> "Today, if you hear his voice,
> do not harden your hearts." (Heb. 4:6–7)

Many people today are dying in their wilderness and don't realize where they are or their spiritual condition. They are actually blind to their unwillingness to truly let the Almighty rule in their lives. One has to wonder how someone could be unaware of his or her stubbornness when it comes to submitting to God's way. That question will be answered with the next basic reason why so many people today die in their wilderness. I believe the best example in the Word to illustrate the next point is found in the book of Numbers and surrounds the sons of Korah:

> Now Korah the son of Izhar, the son of Kohath, the son of Levi, with Dathan and Abiram the sons of Eliab, and On the son of Peleth, sons of Reuben, took men; and they rose up before Moses with some of the children of Israel, two hundred and fifty leaders of the congregation, representatives of the congregation, men of renown. They gathered together against Moses and Aaron, and said to them, "You take too much upon yourselves, for all the congregation is holy, every one of them, and the Lord is among them. Why then do you exalt yourselves above the assembly of the Lord?"
>
> And the Lord spoke to Moses and Aaron, saying, "Separate yourselves from among this congregation, that I may consume them in a moment."
>
> And Moses said: "By this you shall know that the Lord has sent me to do all these works, for I have not done them of my own will." (Num. 16:1–3, 20–21, 28 NKJV)

This account demonstrates how easy it is for so many people to grow stubborn and thus reject the opportunity to learn of or submit to the Almighty's way. They simply convince themselves that the instructions given to them through those whom the Almighty has sent to serve them is not from God. But one cannot dismiss the fact that the Almighty uses people as vehicles to share His Word and to teach others what He would have them know or see. Nevertheless, as the group who came against Moses did in Numbers 16, many today allow themselves to believe that the instrument that God wishes to use must be wrong and their way must be right. The Word issues a warning for us when it comes to this way of thinking:

> Have confidence in your leaders and submit to their authority, because they keep watch over you as those who must give an account. Do this so that their work will be a joy, not a burden, for that would be of no benefit to you. (Heb. 13:17)

And to those with the responsibility of shepherd or messenger, He says the following:

> When I say to a wicked person, "You will surely die," and you do not warn them or speak out to dissuade them from their evil ways in order to save their life, that wicked person will die for their sin, and I will hold you accountable for their blood. But if you do warn the wicked person and they do not turn from their wickedness or from their evil ways, they will die for their sin; but you will have saved yourself.
>
> Again, when a righteous person turns from their righteousness and does evil, and I put a stumbling block before them, they will die. Since you did not warn them, they will die for their sin. The righteous things that person did will not be remembered, and I will hold you accountable for their blood. But if you do warn the righteous person not to sin and they do not sin, they will surely live because they took warning, and you will have saved yourself. (Eze. 3:18–21)

As for getting through the wilderness, Moses was the instrument that the Almighty used to lead the descendants of Israel towards their destination before his passing. If they did not accept what Moses had to say, it stands to reason they were not going to make it to the promised land.

Before moving on, I would like to interject here how God takes care of our needs, even while we are in the wilderness:

> The LORD your God has blessed you in all the work of your hands. He has watched over your journey through this vast wilderness. These forty years the LORD your God has been with you, and you have not lacked anything. (Deut. 2:7)

With that shared, let's now look at another very powerful reason why many suffer a spiritual, and sometimes physical, death in the wilderness today:

> And to whom did God swear that they would never enter his rest if not to those who disobeyed? So we see that they were not able to enter, because of their unbelief. (Heb. 3:18–19)

Now we must understand that the writer of Hebrews was speaking about the descendants of Israel—the same generation of descendants that the Almighty led by night with a pillar of fire and by day with a cloud—the same descendants for whom He opened the Red Sea. So you know they believed He existed. They knew who He was. But many did not believe Him or in Him.

For example, a nation may have a president. The citizens know who the president is, and they know and accept his office or position. But that doesn't mean they believe what he says or believe that he can, or will, do what's in his power to do. Hence, they don't believe in him as their president.

Of course when it comes to human beings, misgivings or lack of faith may be warranted. But that is never the case when it comes to the Almighty. Our heavenly Father makes clear what He wants. However, many who claim to trust and know Him simply don't believe Him. They don't believe what's written in His Word or that He will keep His promises. They also don't believe what His messengers or teachers tell them *if* it conflicts with what they wish or don't wish to do. It is this type of thinking or lack of faith that leads to the following:

> So the LORD's anger was aroused on that day, and He swore an oath, saying, "Surely none of the men who came up from Egypt, from twenty years old and above, shall see the land of which I swore to Abraham, Isaac, and Jacob, because they have not wholly followed Me, except Caleb the son of Jephunneh, the Kenizzite, and Joshua the son of Nun, for they have wholly followed the LORD." So the LORD's anger was aroused against Israel, and He made them wander in the wilderness forty years, until all the generation that had done evil in the sight of the LORD was gone. (Num. 32:10–13 NKJV)

The operative words are "because they have not wholly followed Me." Regrettably, when the Almighty endeavors to convict and convince His children today regarding the same, too many fail to believe the messengers or teachers sent to warn them. Thus they fail to believe God.

The final reason why many drop dead in the wilderness goes hand in hand with unbelief. I believe it to be the saddest reason. Here is where it becomes imperative to discuss step IV.

STEP IV: TESTING

Our time in the wilderness is meant to not only train, purge, and teach us but also to test us. In fact, some make it through the teaching and some the purging; but when it comes to testing, there is one devastating factor that can bring the growing progress to a screeching halt. That factor is *fear*.

In Chapter 13 of Numbers, we see a perfect example of testing in the wilderness. God has delivered the Israelites from Egypt, parted the sea, and provided a pillar of cloud by day and fire by night to lead the Israelites through the wilderness. Yet, after a few men came back from spying out the land God promised, they have this to say:

> We are not able to go up against the people, for they are
> stronger than we. . . . The land through which we have gone as
> spies is a land that devours its inhabitants, and all the people
> whom we saw in it are men of great stature. There we saw the
> giants (the descendants of Anak came from the giants); and
> we were like grasshoppers in our own sight, and so we were in
> their sight. (Num. 13:31–33 NKJV)

Needless to say, those guys did not pass the test. See Numbers 13–14.

In Revelation 21:8, the fearful or the cowardly are the first to be mentioned among those who will spend their eternal existence separated from the Most High. Along with unbelief, fear is an enormous factor in the life of the person who unsuccessfully follows the Christ. Jesus also gave a good example of the crippling effects of fear in his parable about the servant who failed to use his talent due to laziness and his fear of disappointing his master.

Matthew 25:18–19, 24–25, 26–27

But the man who had received one bag went off, dug a hole in the ground and hid his master's money.

> Fear can prevent a child of God from fulfilling his or her God-given purpose.

After a long time the master of those servants returned and settled accounts with them.

Then the man who had received one bag of gold came. "Master," he said, "I knew that you are a hard man, harvesting where you have not sown and gathering where you have not scattered seed. So I was afraid and went out and hid your gold in the ground. See, here is what belongs to you."

His master replied, "You wicked, lazy servant! So you knew that I harvest where I have not sown and gather where I have not scattered seed? Well then, you should have put my money on deposit with the bankers, so that when I returned I would have received it back with interest."

As the master in the parable pointed out, the servant knew him. He knew the master and his expectations well. Yet the servant gave into fear instead of doing what he knew his master required.

Fear can prevent a child of God from fulfilling his or her God-given purpose. It can literally ruin one's life in Him; and as stated above, it goes hand in hand with a lack of belief in the power of our Father in heaven.

However, having the fear is not the problem; giving in to the fear is the problem. The only difference between the coward and the brave is the fact that the brave does what must be done in spite of the fear.

Our belief in the power and Word of the Almighty is absolutely necessary in order to live successfully as a child of God within this mortal age. Therefore we must be tested, for if we do not grow to the point of passing the test on belief and trust in Him, then we have no means for enduring the path we must walk in our fight against evil:

> Every commandment which I command you today you must
> be careful to observe, that you may live and multiply, and go in
> and possess the land of which the Lord swore to your fathers.
> And you shall remember that the Lord your God led you all the
> way these forty years in the wilderness, to humble you and test
> you, to know what was in your heart, whether you would keep
> His commandments or not. (Deut. 8:1–2 NKJV)

First John 5:4 says, "For everyone born of God overcomes the world. This is the victory that has overcome the world, even our faith."

Of course the Almighty already knows what He has placed in us and all that we are capable of. As with everything else He does, the testing is not to benefit Him but His children. It's used to show those with eyes to see and ears to hear where they are in their growth and where they need to be. Throughout our time in our wilderness, our Father tests us to show us what's inside us, so we can know what we need to put off and put on. He tests us so that we can understand our weaknesses, along with our strengths, to assist us with our practice to live righteous lives each day.

A perfect example of this is found in Numbers 14:11–20 when the Almighty threatens to destroy all of Israel except Moses. Did the Almighty actually need counsel from Moses? Did this mortal have more foresight and wisdom than Almighty God? Of course not, but it served not only as a test for Moses but also to leave us an example of what would be accomplished by our Intercessor to come (i.e., the Christ).

Our Father knows and understands that we cannot fight an enemy we cannot see, be it without or within us. Therefore, He tests us so that we can know where we are in our ability to believe and trust Him and where we are in the transformation of our character as we strive each day to live in this world as disciples of the Christ.

So what if, after reading this chapter, you come to realize that you've been in the wilderness for years due to stubbornness, rebellion, or unbelief. What happens now? The fact is, it does not matter to the Almighty what one has done *if* he or she is truly regretful and follows His process of confessing and forsaking whatever the person's done. When we truly wish to change, and long for the opportunity to start over, He forgives us and gives us that opportunity because forgiveness from God means "forgotten."

Isaiah 43:25

I, even I, am He who blots out
>your transgressions, for my own sake,
>and remembers your sins no more.

Ezekiel 18:23

Do I take any pleasure in the death of the wicked? declares the Sovereign LORD. Rather, am I not pleased when they turn from their ways and live?

Micah 7:18

Who is a God like you,

who pardons sin and forgives the transgression

of the remnant of his inheritance?

You do not stay angry forever

but delight to show mercy.

All of the foregoing scriptures reveal His position before His Son sat at His right hand to make intercession for us. So how much greater is His willingness to forgive now that His Son has paid the price for us.

You may be wondering, *What if I am married and my spouse is in the wilderness, but God knows that I'm ready to come out?* Not to worry—the Almighty is just. He is definitely known for showing favor to an entire household due to the obedience of one person—remember Noah?

For those who are now aware that they are still wandering in the wilderness, I would recommend you read 2 Timothy 1:7, along with Hebrews 5:11–15 and Hebrews chapter 12.

8

THE PROCESS

STEP V: POSSESSION

Let's move on to the last and final step we take during this transient age. Step five is only experienced by those who have successfully taken the first four steps. It's important to understand that with the Almighty there are no shortcuts.

This step consists of entering the land flowing with milk and honey (Deut. 26:9). However, before entering this land you have to go up and take it. In other words, since you are now well acquainted with the Almighty and His ways, it's time to put what you've learned to good use while laying hold of what's in store for you through what remains of your mortal existence.

You've passed your initial tests. Now you, along with the holy host of heaven, know that you are committed and that you practice righteousness daily while striving to be obedient and led by the guidance and teachings of the Christ. The Almighty can now trust you with certain responsibilities based on your particular gifts, temperament, and individuality.

This final step of the process is the end of basic training for children of God. Here's where they come into their own. It is now expected of them to take the wings they've acquired by way of their perseverance, submissiveness, and obedience and fly. In other words, it's time for you to fulfill your individual purpose in Him, to further develop and exercise your God-given gifts.

> And I have promised to bring you up out of your misery in Egypt into the land of the Canaanites, Hittites, Amorites, Perizzites, Hivites, and Jebusites—a land flowing with milk and honey. (Ex. 3:17)

Just as the Israelites had to confront the Canaanites, Hittites, Amorites, Perizzites, Hivites, and Jebusites, you, too, have come face-to-face with your greatest enemies—the enemies within you. The Almighty has worked and fought along with you to attack those inner enemies (pride, fear, selfishness). You've destroyed some and brought others under submission; now you are free to move forward.

You have come face-to-face with your greatest enemies—the enemies within you.

Having had your mind renewed and purged from the ways of the opposer and the world while in the wilderness, as an obedient, submissive child of God you are now free to be the person the Almighty has raised and trained you to be. Of course you will continue to learn and be tested to keep you on your toes, but you are now trustworthy enough to be used in the work of your Father in heaven, according to His purpose.

Since the land you've entered is one flowing with milk and honey, you will also experience more of the things that will bring you joy or fulfillment in different areas of your life.

For when a person truly and sincerely seeks "first the kingdom of God and His righteousness" (Matt. 6:33 NKJV) daily, the Almighty takes care of all his or her physical needs and then some.

> Now to him who is able to do immeasurably more than all we ask or imagine, according to his power that is at work within us, to him be glory in the church and in Christ Jesus throughout all generations, for ever and ever! Amen. (Eph.3:20–21)

However, it's important to stress that taking this final step does not mean that you won't make mistakes or that you've learned all you need to know. But you need to understand that mistakes, offenses, or trespasses are not deliberate sin or transgression.

1 John 5:18–20 (NKJV)
We know that whoever is born of God does not sin; but he who has been born of God keeps himself, and the wicked one does not touch him. We know that we are of God, and the whole world lies under the sway of the wicked one. And we know that the Son of God has come and has given us an understanding, that we may know Him who is true; and we are in Him who is true, in His Son Jesus Christ. This is the true God and eternal life.

Hebrews 10:26
If we deliberately keep on sinning after we have received the knowledge of the truth, no sacrifice for sins is left.

Do not be deceived—at this stage of growth, first-degree deliberate transgression or sin against the Almighty should no longer be an issue. To sit and contemplate doing something one knows opposes our Father in heaven is impossible for a truly obedient, loving, and submissive child of God.

There are many who profess to be Christians who do not accept this truth, nor do they believe it possible. Thereby, they limit the Almighty Sovereign of the universe. In fact, there are certain doctrines that teach that living without deliberate sin is impossible. It's one of the reasons why the United States is in its current condition, in spite of the fact that more than 70 percent of its citizens profess to be Christians. It's why there are so many who can identify with the title of this book.

The Almighty Creator who made the sun, moon, earth, and everything else created therein, including human beings, is certainly capable of enabling, or giving one who longs not to deliberately disobey Him the power to conquer deliberate sin.

Though one may disobey Him during a time of sudden emotional stress or under unidentified or uncontrollable physical weakness, no one at this stage of *His* process, who truly loves, cherishes, and appreciates Him for who and what He is can deliberately hurt Him.

In our next chapter, we will discuss the level of growth, knowledge, understanding, and wisdom one can expect to develop throughout stage five of the process.

9

DISCERNING AND GROWING

One of the most challenging and perhaps frustrating experiences for a child of the Almighty is learning to discern correctly the will of our Father in each area of our lives. There are three extremely important prerequisites to developing the ability to discern His will or His point of view regarding the issues and circumstances we face daily. They are:

1. Removing the beam from our own eyes so we can see things as they are, not as we want them to be;
2. Accepting what we see once it's been shown to us;
3. Walking in the light we receive by exercising numbers 1 and 2.

Removing the Beam

The Christ said in Matthew 7:3–4, "Why do you look at the speck of sawdust in your brother's eye and pay no attention to the plank in your own eye? How can you say to your brother, 'Let me take the speck out of your eye,' when all the time there is a plank in your own eye?"

In His analogy of the splinter and the beam, the Christ spoke of the beam as an obstacle that prevents a person from seeing what needs to be seen. In other words, the beam hinders the individual from seeing things as they truly are. He said, "First take the plank out of your own eye, and then you will see clearly to remove the speck from your brother's eye" (Matt. 7:5).

Therefore, removing the beam does not always remove the issue(s) a person needs to face. But it would enable one to see clearly the issue or problem and what's needed for correction or healing. With that insight, one can gain the understanding necessary to help himself and others.

Facing the truth is one of the biggest stumbling blocks believers encounter. God's children who desire to walk the path He designated struggle with this often, especially when it comes to the truth regarding the filthy residue from their own past or decisions. However, in order to remove the beam we must first accept its existence and that it's preventing us from seeing our own issues. In other words, we must be honest with ourselves.

As human beings, this seems to be one of the greatest challenges we face, particularly if a great change will be required in our lives or if we will experience a dreadful awakening regarding what or who we believe ourselves to be. The apostle John, in chapter 3 of his gospel, said:

> This is the verdict: Light has come into the world, but people loved darkness instead of light because their deeds were evil. Everyone who does evil hates the light, and will not come into the light for fear that their deeds will be exposed. But whoever lives by the truth comes into the light, so that it may be seen plainly that what they have done has been done in the sight of God, (vv. 19–21)

Accepting the Light

It is absolutely amazing what human beings are capable of thinking and doing in order to maintain a false impression of themselves and their lives. However, there are those who find it hard to ignore the truth regarding who or what or where they are. So they choose to use drugs, alcohol, or some other type of substance or habit to escape the truth rather than turn to God.

A child of God has to come to the knowledge and understanding that the goal is to become like Jesus, who, when on earth, thought and did exactly as His Father would if He lived among us in a mortal body.

True transformation requires that we tear down the old so we can build up the new. But we cannot renovate a house without first looking at what needs to be repaired, replaced, or replenished. This of course coincides with Jesus's teachings about the old and the new, for He taught:

> *True transformation requires that we tear down the old so we can build up the new.*

> No one sews a patch of unshrunk cloth on an old garment, for the patch will pull away from the garment, making the tear worse. Neither do people pour new wine into old wineskins. If they do, the skins will burst; the wine will run out and the wineskins will be ruined. No, they pour new wine into new wineskins, and both are preserved. (Matt. 9:16–17)

Another big obstacle is the inability to humble ourselves. Humility is the flashlight needed to take an honest look at our inner household. We need it because it can be pretty dark in there. When Jesus said "A man's enemies will be the members of his own household" (Matt. 10:36). I believe that He was not just referring to outer members and influences in our lives but to those who live within us where we are supposed to permit the Almighty to set up rule. We have to make room for His reign in our lives, and we can't do that if we don't take an honest look at the things that get in the way.

> Another big obstacle is the inability to humble ourselves.

Of course, we need the Almighty's Word and Holy Spirit (His enabling power) to accomplish that. But even with all He provides, as with any renovation, we cannot do it all at once. Nevertheless, the first step is to be honest enough with ourselves to accept the work that has to be done and the reality that it's a great big mess. That's exactly what we are when we come to Him—a mess. Therefore, we must be honest about it by removing the "beam" and looking closely at anything that could keep us from accepting what has to be purged and cleansed from within us. If we fail to do this, we will inevitably continue to be a mess (i.e., those of us who see or produce very little progress, growth, or real change in our lives).

Humility is paramount, there's no room for pride in this process. Still, many professing Christians have a terrible time with anyone pointing out their "speck." They find the truth offensive. For a successful child of God, this type of attitude is unacceptable and disruptive.

Rebuke or reproof is not pleasant. Yet even by the world's standards, individuals who become the best at what they do all had past mentors or teachers whom they would say were very hard on them and brutally truthful with them.

If we look at Jesus's example of His time with His disciples, we don't find him sugarcoating the truth. He had a great deal to teach them in a limited amount of time, and He took every opportunity to do just that.

Again, Solomon points out the value of both rebuke and reproof and the benefits of listening to the wise (see Proverbs 5:13; Ecclesiastes 7:5).

Yet in today's Western society, the concept of learning from elders or mentors is rare. Most people wish to be the "chief." Those people call mentorship the "authoritarian approach," and treat it as a relic they have the option to dismiss and replace. There's no doubt that some people with authority in our lives have abused that authority, but that does not justify throwing the baby out with the bathwater, so to speak.

We only have to look at the condition of our Western world today to see that passive parenting and the advocating of resistance to authority was a mistake. It's taught human beings to not respect or submit to authority, rather than teaching them how to discern which authorities can be trusted.

The fact is, the Almighty is the final authority. However, throughout this transient age, He always has, and always will, use humans to teach other humans. If one has been taught to rebel against the authority he or she can see, one is going to have a hard time submitting to an authority he or she can't see. John said, "If someone says, "I love God," and hates his brother, he is a liar; for he who does not love his brother whom he has seen, how can[a] he love God whom he has not seen? (1 John 4:20 NKJV).

As obedient children of God, we have to maintain an open ear to the truth. Especially when offered knowledge, wisdom, or insight from those who have gone or are going before us, even when it comes in the form of rebuke or reproof. Humility is not synonymous with being a doormat. It's simply accepting the truth regarding one's strengths and weaknesses. It's taking responsibility for our actions and accepting our consequences without anger or defensiveness and our rewards and accomplishments without pride. Humility allows us to accept the light (the truth) no matter where it comes from.

Walking in the Light

Those of us who have raised or are still raising children know that as they live and grow we teach and expose them to different things. Virtually on a daily basis we expose them to something, or many things, they must learn.

For example, a situation may arise where the child lies, so the importance of telling the truth and the consequences of lying may be pointed out to him or her. In that same day that same child may say something mean or cruel to a sibling, so knowledge regarding gentleness and kindness may be shared. Again, within the same day, that child may neglect to fulfill a responsibility, and the importance of keeping one's word and being responsible may be stressed.

The age of the child, the importance or consequences of an action(s), or how often it's been addressed should determine the manner in which a parent or guardian handles situations when they occur. Nevertheless, once the child has been given knowledge and understanding regarding any subject matter, behavior, and so forth, would it be acceptable to a parent or guardian for that child to determine that he or she does not plan to apply what's been shown or taught—until the child feels like it?

For instance, you know the child is of an age in which he or she understands what's expected. But it is apparent the child feels that he or she should not have to put forth the effort it takes to apply what has been taught until the child feels more comfortable with it or deems it necessary.

What if the child simply determines that it's just not a high enough priority in life—right now—to apply certain things that have been taught to him or her, regardless of the consequences?

I believe it would be safe to say that this type of thinking or attitude from a son or daughter would be unacceptable. We as parents or guardians expect our children to make use of what we've taught them as situations or opportunities arise.

For example, the next time a sibling does something your eldest child disapproves of, he or she is expected to handle the situation as you taught him or her. When the time comes for the child to fulfill a particular responsibility, you expect the child to get it done. It would be unacceptable to you, as a parent or guardian, for your child to tell you, "I hear you, and I plan to get to that, but I have to do it once I think I'm ready."

We teach our children so that they have the knowledge they will need to deal with different situations as they arise. If we are wise parents, we understand that the more we help them to put what they learn into practice, the sooner those things will become a part of them. They can then move on to deeper and more important knowledge to prepare them for adulthood.

> So many times, professing Christians do with God what we would find unacceptable from our own children.

So many times, professing Christians do with God what we would find unacceptable from our own children or what we would not do with our biological parents. When the Almighty gives us light (i.e., knowledge or understanding regarding those things that are beneficial for our lives or for those within our lives), too many of us take the attitude, "Well, I'm not there

yet," or "I can't do everything at once." It's true: we cannot do everything at once. It would be impossible to do so. Physically, we can only take one day at a time, taking advantage of each opportunity as it comes. However, Jesus said, "You are going to have the light just a little while longer. Walk while you have the light, before darkness overtakes you. Whoever walks in the dark does not know where they are going. Believe in the light while you have the light, so that you may become children of light" (John 12:35–38).

The reason it is so important to walk in the light (i.e., to accept and then fight to put on, apply, or practice what you received) is simply because when we put off doing so, it leaves an opening for deception to creep into our thinking and into our lives. It is extremely important, at all times, for a child of God to be aware of the powers that be and the workings of those entities of the unseen world, especially those who oppose our Father.

Yes, our Father uses His power and resources, such as His Son, His Word, the Holy Spirit, and the guardians placed with each and every one of His obedient children (His workers, the angels) to guide and influence our thoughts and decisions. However, though far inferior in power and knowledge, His opposers and archenemy also have resources and those who work for them.

What we've seen on television of the angel and the "devil" whispering in the ear of an individual, influencing their decisions, is not far from the truth.

Therefore, when the Almighty gives us light, be it through a human being, His Word, the Holy Spirit, or by the use of His angels, if we choose to not walk in it, we are left open for opposing forces to influence our thinking. As a result, we blindly begin falsely justifying or thinking in ways that will absolutely hinder the very growth we need to achieve.

A child of God who willingly takes on the attitude or thinks that he or she has the right to put *on hold* the light the Almighty provides not only hinders his or her growth but also risks spending years on the path to bearing little or no fruit (review chapter 6).

God will not be mocked. What He shared with us through Jesus's teachings is truth, and when we don't walk in that truth, we reap the consequences. The Bible says, "Be alert and of sober mind. Your enemy the devil prowls around like a roaring lion looking for someone to devour" (1 Pet. 5:8). Moreover, he and his forces are very skillful at what they do.

Therefore, as children of God, we cannot afford to purposely put off light when it is revealed to us. What may seem like a little thing at the time can lead to so much and affect so many.

We understand how children (spiritual or physical) who are growing and learning may forget or miss opportunities or, in a moment of great emotional weakness or through ignorance, make a mistake or fall short of what they know is right and good to do. But to intentionally take on the attitude that basically says "I can't do but so much," or "I have to take baby steps—I can't do it all at once" is actually saying to your Father in heaven, "You can't enable me to do what you say I should do, or "I only wish to put forth a certain amount of effort for you or anyone. I have to do what works for me." In other words, you limit the Almighty Sovereign of heaven and earth and hinder your ability to make use of the power He gives to all those who wish to grow and become what He would have them become.

The ability to submit to God's knowledge and understanding, regardless of the source, requires that you long for the truth, His way of thinking, His knowledge, and His understanding. And you must long for it more than what makes you feel comfortable, more than what you are accustomed to— more than anything. It also requires that when the thought(s) comes to you to do what you know is good and right to do, *you just do it,* trusting Him to enable you.

Jesus has taught us that *if we ask our Father in heaven for anything according to His decrees He* will *do it.* Surely it is our Father's wish that we trust and obey Him and take advantage of His knowledge, wisdom, and understanding.

> Jesus has taught us that *if we ask our Father in Heaven for anything according to His decrees He* will *do it.*

For most of us, there are, or have been, individuals whom God has used in our lives—people He used to share many things we needed to see, or realize, as we continue to grow and develop the ability to see more on our own—or we may have colleagues within the holy kindred to help us discern. If these individuals exist in your life, then according to your longing for the truth, trust that the Almighty can and will use them for the furtherance of your growth.

However, if a person really does not wish to know, he or she has a tendency not to take advantage of sources that might reveal what he or she does not wish to see or accept. It is only through fighting against what feels comfortable and doing what we've been taught is good and right to do, in spite of what we feel, that we can become what He would have us to become. It's called *endurance.* The Word makes it perfectly clear that it's only through endurance that we can achieve growth as a child of God. Read what Jesus taught regarding the sower and the seed in Matthew 13:1–23.

There will be plenty of time for rest in the new age to come when His Sovereignty fills the whole earth. But for now, as those who have been called and chosen by God, we have work to do and goals to reach, awesome goals:

- to follow daily the example left us by Jesus;
- to grow as one with God in character, how we think, the choices we make—just as the Christ was one with Him in all things;
- to prepare for the age to come by seeking daily His kingdom and righteousness;
- to be lights (manifest God) to those in this world, especially those still living in darkness;
- to be good examples and leaders to those for whom we have been given responsibility, especially the children in our lives, be they our own or those whom our lives influence.

Understand, it is impossible to apply everything at once. Growth is just that, *growth*. The very definition for growth according to *Readers Digest Dictionary* follows: "the act, or process of growing: advancement toward or attainment of full size or maturity; development."

Praise the Almighty that life as a human does not require, or even permit, us to do everything at once:

> Therefore do not worry about tomorrow, for tomorrow will worry about itself. Each day has enough trouble of its own. (Matt. 6:34)

When it comes to what we are to put on and put off in our lives, or when it comes to righteousness, wisdom, or anything pertaining to our growth as children of God, we only have to live one day at a time, taking advantage of each opportunity as it comes. However, an obedient child of God simply cannot take those days for granted. Be it situations, relationships, needs, challenges, or opportunities, we cannot afford to get caught up with what the world throws our way. We cannot allow ourselves to forget who we are, our goals, and purpose as sojourners in this world. Furthermore, we should be greatly appreciative of the new knowledge and understanding (light) the Almighty permits us to receive. We should take advantage of those opportunities by applying that knowledge and understanding wherever or whenever opportunities arise.

Hence is a true life in the Christ. It may sound like a lot, but we only have to take one day at a time. The great news is, when we consistently practice living His way, it becomes habit, and we just flow with it in freedom and in peace. It's a wonderful way to live, regardless of what trials, hardships, or changes we may endure.

In closing this chapter, it is important to remember the fact that we are to simply accept what's given to us (i.e., the Almighty's truth and wisdom) and then trust Him to enable us to remember and apply it when necessary. For there may be times when we feel overwhelmed as our Father is using someone or something to teach or enlighten us.

As a side note, I'd like to share something I've observed as my body approaches seniorhood. I find myself with an even greater appreciation for how fearfully and marvelously God has made us. For it appears that our bodies age in proportion to our spiritual growth, or at least what it should be. It seems that the weakness or lack of energy we experience as our bodies grow older actually aids us in our ability to be swift to hear and slow to speak. We lack the energy to fall into certain mistakes and find more time to think and reflect on our actions.

Think about it. Though we get in enough trouble while young and full of energy, imagine how much more damage we could cause if by the age of ten we understood how to effectively deceive, manipulate, or finagle? That type of knowledge and ability, coupled with the immaturity and energy of youth, would reap far more consequences than is common among children. So though we may find ourselves thinking of what we could do with all that energy, it would seem that it is as it should be.

If my observation is correct, then it can serve as further proof regarding the process and time it takes to reach maturity as a child of God. The fact is, it takes a lifetime—a lifetime consisting of daily commitment, growth, and everything else we've discussed in the previous chapters.

Growth is not a comfortable experience, if for no other reason than it requires discipline. But as it is written, "Now no chastening seems to be joyful for the present, but painful; nevertheless, afterward it yields the peaceable fruit of righteousness to those who have been trained by it" (Hebrews 12:11 NKJV).

> Growth is not a comfortable experience, if for no other reason than it requires discipline.

Right now, we are in God's Holy College of Righteousness, and the goal is to graduate with honors; only we really cannot afford to be kept back a grade. To fall short could reap irrevocable consequences. The good news is, He never holds us back—we hold ourselves back.

10

THE FUTURE

Before bringing this book to a conclusion, I thought it fitting to talk about the future as it pertains to children of God. Regardless of where one is in the process, it is important that a child of God see the future in line with the truth.

Most people are under the mistaken impression that they are in control of their lives. People of the world give very little thought to the unseen forces that really run the show. Many will choose not to submit to God's rule based on the belief that by doing so they have the freedom to plan their own future and determine their own way or destiny. They believe to have the Almighty rule their lives is to face a future of uncertainty.

This belief is a huge deception; need I say from where? The fact is, a child of the Almighty has far more foresight into the future than one who is unconverted. In fact, the unconverted can kiss their plans good-bye if the force to which they've chosen to submit (the opposer of the Almighty) determines that it will be disruptive to his agenda.

The scary part is, it may not be the only thing they kiss good-bye, because the manner in which the opposer may choose to stop or thwart their plans could be disastrous, or worse. This is one of the reasons why it appears that bad things happen to good people when those people are the unconverted.

Yes, it appears that bad things can happen to children of God also. Though, when faced with these "bad things," one should honestly ask "Was there any action or choice I made to contribute to my circumstances?" Too often, professing Christians want to blame the "devil" for choices they make.

God is trustworthy. He keeps His Word. His committed children, through their obedience and the fact that they already live according to His purpose need not have the same concerns as the unconverted. Once we truly belong to the Almighty, we can be assured that we will not encounter many of the evils in the world that fall upon the unconverted, because we are obedient children of the Most High, and strive each day to live life as He intended:

> **Psalm 37:25**
> I was young and now I am old,
> > yet I have never seen the righteous forsaken
> > or their children begging bread.

> **Proverbs 3:21–26**
> My son, do not let wisdom and understanding out of your sight,
> > preserve sound judgment and discretion;
> they will be life for you,
> > an ornament to grace your neck.
> Then you will go on your way in safety, and your foot will not stumble.
> When you lie down, you will not be afraid;
> > when you lie down, your sleep will be sweet.
> Have no fear of sudden disaster
> > or of the ruin that overtakes the wicked,
> for the Lord will be at your side
> > and will keep your foot from being snared.

The Creator has not changed. However, when it comes to the obedient children of God, He has shown us in His Word how when their bodies died of what might be thought of as a horrible death or they were made to endure a terrible experience, He prepared them for it. His children would not only know it was coming, they would also have knowledge, or learn afterwards why it occurred. Also, sometimes there is the need for a great and valuable lesson to be taught (see the book of Job) or to get the attention of one who is ignoring the Almighty's "pricks" (see Acts 9:1-6). When this occurs, He may wait until after the event to shed light.

In other words, there has always been a lesson or greater purpose for anything and everything that occurs in the life of an *obedient* child of God. Even when those things consist of persecution, torture, or worse.

However, His history with the Israelites makes it absolutely clear that disaster, pain, or sorrow can definitely come upon one claiming to belong to Him if he or she is living in disobedience. One is also vulnerable if he or she falls into disobedience without immediately confessing and forsaking the transgression or trespass. But in the case of disobedience, the Almighty always issues a warning in order to give His children the opportunity to repent, though many times His warnings are ignored.

> There has always been a lesson, or greater purpose for anything and everything that occurs in the life of an *obedient* child of God.

In the book of Joshua, before going up to conquer the city of Jericho, the men were warned to keep away from the devoted things, so not to bring about their own destruction and make the camp of Israel subject to

destruction also. But one man, Achan, did not take heed to the warning. Achan's disobedience brought about a great defeat for the men of Israel. Without knowing the cause for the defeat, Joshua's first response was doubt and remorse for even attempting to take the city. But after speaking with God about it, He told Joshua that Israel could not stand before their enemies until they took away the devoted things from among them.

After God's process of elimination among the tribes of Israel, it was brought to light that it was Achan who had disobeyed. He, along with his family (as was the custom and law) were then stoned to death (see Joshua 7).

In this account from the book of Joshua, we see how one act of disobedience caused defeat and fear for the Almighty's people. However, Joshua's first thought was that it was a mistake to reach for the goal in the first place. This is often the same conclusion God's people draw today when things go wrong or not as they hoped.

When something goes wrong regarding a goal or task that we sought His counsel about and prayed over, the first thing we should examine is ourselves. Are we now, or have we been, obedient? Did we go about it in obedience?

Obedience and submission to the Almighty is all that matters in life, for in doing so we can discern and fulfill His purpose for our lives. When we live in obedience, then we can walk in confidence, secure in our relationship with the Almighty as we trust in the same words He shared with Joshua:

> Be strong and very courageous. Be careful to obey all the law
> my servant Moses gave you; do not turn from it to the right or
> to the left, that you may be successful wherever you go. Keep
> this Book of the Law always on your lips; meditate on it day
> and night, so that you may be careful to do everything written

in it. Then you will be prosperous and successful. Have I not commanded you? Be strong and courageous. Do not be afraid; do not be discouraged, for the LORD your God will be with you wherever you go. (Josh. 1:7–9)

Regarding the law, the Christ taught us how we should think and what we should do when it comes to the law today:

Love the Lord your God with all your heart and with all your soul, and with all your mind. This is the first and greatest commandment. And the second is like it: Love your neighbor as yourself. All the Law and the Prophets hang on these two commandments. (Matt. 22:37–40)

As for the daily challenges we face in life due to our weaknesses as mortals, and the evil in the world—we must exercise our faith in *Him*. With confidence, God's obedient children can rest under His protection and trustworthiness when it comes to anything that could disrupt His plan or purpose for our lives. It's also needless to say, that as long as we live within mortal bodies, we needn't know everything that will occur before it happens. Yet, when it comes to knowing what the future will bring, God's children are in a far better position than those who are unconverted. Because every child of God knows for certain what his or her ultimate future holds. Each will receive his or her inheritance, which includes the earth and everything else our Creator made.

Below is the light I received long ago. I think it serves as a perfect example of how a child of God can reason when faced with certain *temporary* limitations:

Once I thought about how I never mastered the violin. I then went on to think of how it was too late, that there was not enough time. Then the thought came to me that I had eternity. Therefore, I was not bound by the same limitations as those without eternal security; those who are pressed to squeeze everything they wish to do, see, or accomplish within their body's life span, while having no idea how long that might be.

Once I receive the immortal body God will give me, I will have eternity to master the violin. I can then master the flute and then the harp or guitar, perhaps all at the same time. Once I am done with mastering what I wish to master in the realm of music, I can go on to master the sciences and other arts, and the list can go on and on forever.

Unlike the unconverted of the world, who don't seem to look any further than what they see here and now, a child of God knows that everything made by humans was made with what the Creator had already provided. Therefore, it all belongs to Him, and He plans to give everything to His children as an inheritance.

Surely that's worth subduing one's body. Surely a life filled with peace, and the joy that comes from the unity and security one can have with the Almighty and His Son now and forevermore, is worth anything and everything. If one thinks it's not worth whatever he or she may need to endure during this temporary existence within the body, Jesus and Paul had something to say on the subject.

Matthew 10:37–39; 16:26–27

Anyone who loves their father or mother more than me is not worthy of me; anyone who loves their son or daughter more than me is not worthy of me. Whoever does not take up their cross and follow me is not worthy of me. Whoever finds their life will lose it, and whoever loses their life for my sake will find it.

What good will it be for someone to gain the whole world, yet forfeit their soul? Or what can anyone give in exchange for their soul? For the Son of Man is going to come in his Father's glory with his angels, and then he will reward each person according to what they have done.

Romans 8:17–21

Now if we are children, then we are heirs—heirs of God and co-heirs with Christ, if indeed we share in his sufferings in order that we may also share in his glory.

I consider that our present sufferings are not worth comparing with the glory that will be revealed in us. For the creation waits in eager expectation for the children of God to be revealed. For the creation was subjected to frustration, not by its own choice, but by the will of the one who subjected it, in hope that the creation itself will be liberated from its bondage to decay and brought into the freedom and glory of the children of God.

At this point, I feel it is necessary to stress again what we discussed in previous chapters because it is so important to understand what's required of the believer: we are to simply turn our lives over to the Almighty with a determination to do things His way and to become who and what He intended. That does not mean that we are instantly free of the bad habits, programming, memories, impulses, inclinations, or ways of thinking that we accumulated before conversion. Our choice to follow His Son, and to commit to living life according to the Almighty's purpose, frees us from the transgressions or sins we've committed against Him and their eternal consequences. It also places us in a position to attend the school of God so that we can be taught, trained, and groomed to represent the Almighty as His children (i.e., holy royalty).

However, a purging process is involved in which every child of God must participate and endure in order to become free from those old habits, programming, memories, impulses, inclinations, ways of thinking, and so forth.

His process is one that will take your entire mortal life. But in order to live successfully as a child of God, you must submit to and endure it:

> And you have forgotten the exhortation which speaks to you as to sons:

> "My son, do not despise the chastening of the LORD,
> Nor be discouraged when you are rebuked by Him;
> For whom the LORD loves He chastens,
> And scourges every son whom He receives."

> If you endure chastening, God deals with you as with sons; for what son is there whom a father does not chasten? But if you are without chastening, of which all have become partakers, then you are illegitimate and not sons. Furthermore, we

have had human fathers who corrected us, and we paid them respect. Shall we not much more readily be in subjection to the Father of spirits and live? For they indeed for a few days chastened us as seemed best to them, but He for our profit, that we may be partakers of His holiness. Now no chastening seems to be joyful for the present, but painful; nevertheless, afterward it yields the peaceable fruit of righteousness to those who have been trained by it. (Heb. 12:5–11 NKJV)

Now you know what His process is.

For those of you to whom the primary title of this book applies, now you should know what has hindered your growth. Now you should have some insight regarding what's kept you from fulfilling your purpose and living the life you can, and should, have in Jesus.

Now you know. Do you accept it? If so, will you walk in His light? With love and caring concern I pray you do. He loves you, and He wants you to know true freedom. His Son made His mission clear to His disciples: "I have come that they may have life and have it to the full" (John 10:10).

Time is running out, and His plan is coming to a head. Even if His Son should tarry, you have no idea when time will cease to exist for your mortal body. So don't give yourself anymore excuses; don't try to convince yourself that this whole book is about earning your salvation. Nothing could be further from the truth. The truth is, once we have accepted the gift of reconciliation with God, we are to use all that He has given us to live a life worthy of His calling. So stop accepting any lie that can contribute to a defeated life, and live the life He intended for you. Let yourself experience true growth and power in Him.

OTHER BOOKS FROM AUTHOR

MORIEL RANDOLPH

For more information about the author, her blog, and ministry, please visit:
what-is-the-truth-today.com
or you can find her on Facebook:

https://www.facebook.com/Author-MoriEl-Randolph-2054949661398224/

and on Twitter:
https://twitter.com/Salvation_Help

You can also email the author @
author@freshviewbooks.com